Everyday Science Experiments
Fizz in the Kitchen

Susan Martineau
Illustrated by Leighton Noyes

with thanks to Kathryn Higgins,
Head of Chemistry, Leighton Park School

WINDMILL BOOKS
New York

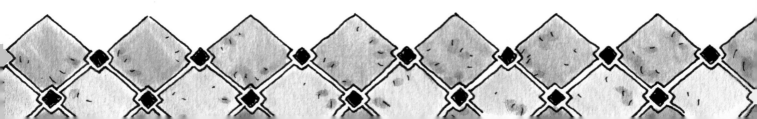

Published in 2012 by Windmill Books, An Imprint of Rosen Publishing
29 East 21st Street, New York, NY 10010

© 2012 b small publishing ltd
Adaptations to North American Edition © 2012 Windmill Books, An Imprint of Rosen Publishing

Library of Congress Cataloging-in-Publication Data

Martineau, Susan.
Fizz in the kitchen / by Susan Martineau. — 1st ed.
p. cm. — (Everyday science experiments)
Includes index.
ISBN 978-1-61533-373-8 (library binding) — ISBN 978-1-61533-411-7 (pbk.) —
ISBN 978-1-61533-482-7 (6-pack)
1. Food – Composition – Juvenile literature. 2. Chemistry,
Technical – Experiments – Juvenile literature. 1. Title.
TX541.M37 2012
664 – dc22
2010052122

Manufactured in the United States of America

CPSIA Compliance Information: Batch #BS2011WM: For Further Information contact Windmill Books, New York, New York at 1-866-478-0556

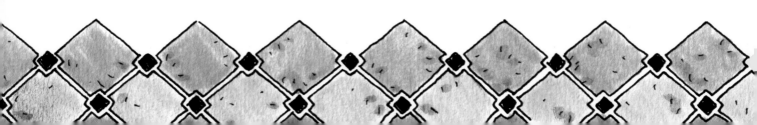

contents

How to Be a Scientist

One way that scientists learn about the world is by doing experiments. You will learn about the science in your kitchen in this book. You shouldn't need to buy anything for these experiments. You'll probably have most of the things you'll need in your kitchen already. Don't forget to ask a grown-up if you can use things, though. Before you begin an experiment, always read it all the way through to make sure you have everything you need.

BE SAFE!

Ask a grown-up to give you a hand when you are heating or cutting things.

Bubble Trouble!

Soft drinks have loads of bubbles in them. These bubbles are there because a gas was mixed into the liquid. You can have some fun with these bubbles. A clear soft drink will work better than a cola. It will let you can see what is happening.

1. Pour some clear soft drink into a glass.

2. Drop a handful of raisins into the liquid.

3. Watch what happens to the raisins.

Let's Take a Closer Look!

The bubbles of **gas** in the drink stick to the raisins. The gas is lighter than the **liquid**, so it rises to the top of the glass, carrying the raisins with it. The bubbles then pop and the raisins sink back down. Then more bubbles stick to them and up they go again!

Did You Know?

Other foods also have gas bubbles in them. The holes inside cupcakes, muffins, and breads are made by gas bubbles, too.

Quick Quiz!

Can you find out the name of this gas?
Clue: Look on page 9.

The Big Fizz

Expect some bubbling fun with this experiment. You will need to place the glass in a shallow dish or the sink to catch any overflowing foam. Please don't put your face too near the glass. The fizz gets very stinky!

1. Put 1 tablespoon of baking soda in a large glass.

2. Place the glass in a dish.

3. Pour 2 tablespoons of vinegar into a small pitcher.

4. Pour the vinegar over the baking soda.

Let's Take a Closer Look!

The baking soda and the vinegar are different types of chemicals. When they are mixed, something called a **chemical reaction** happens. The reaction makes a gas called **carbon dioxide**. This causes all the bubbling and fizzing.

Wash everything down the sink when you're done.

Try This!

Use a funnel to put some baking soda inside a balloon. Put some vinegar in a small bottle and carefully put the balloon over the bottle's neck. Watch the balloon blow up as the baking soda and vinegar react.

Quick Warning!

Make sure not to get the vinegar near your eyes. It can sting.

Air Power

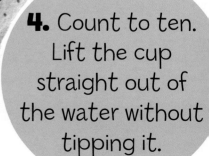

Trick your friends with this experiment.
No one will believe that it will work.
All you need is the kitchen sink, a plastic cup,
a paper towel, and the air around you!

1. Push the paper towel firmly into the bottom of the cup.

2. Fill the sink with water.

3. Turn the cup upside down. Hold it straight and push it down into the water.

4. Count to ten. Lift the cup straight out of the water without tipping it.

Quick Quiz!

What is the name of the gas our bodies need to breathe?

Clue: You'll find its name on this page.

Did You Know?

The air around us is a mixture of gases. The main ones are called nitrogen and oxygen. Most gases are invisible. They still take up space as the air in your cup did, though.

Let's Take a Closer Look!

Amazingly, the paper towel does not get wet. No water gets into the cup because the cup is already full of air. You cannot see it, but this air is taking up space inside the cup. There is no room for the water to get in.

Quick Fact

Some gases are very smelly. One, called hydrogen sulfide, smells like rotten eggs!

oily Stuff

Oil and water do not mix. If you try to mix oil with water, you will see that when you stop stirring, the oil stays on the top, or surface, of the water. If you add some dish soap to the water, though, something very interesting happens.

1. Pour some water into a bowl.

2. Add some cooking oil.

3. Now add some drops of dish soap and stir the water

When was the last time you did the dishes?

Did You Know?

Birds have a sort of oil smeared on their feathers. It keeps them waterproof so that they don't get soaking wet in the rain or on a pond.

Quick Fact

Oil from oil tankers sometimes spills into seas and oceans. This oil is very bad for seabirds. It floats on the top of the water and can kill them and other sea creatures.

Get those greasy dishes clean with some dish soap!

Let's Take a Closer Look!

The drops of oil float on top of the water. They have a kind of stretchy skin around them and they like to stick together. The dish soap breaks up the skin and helps the oil and water mix together.

Waterworks

When you turn on the faucet, clean water for drinking, cooking, and washing comes pouring out. Before it reaches us, water has to be cleaned, or filtered, to get rid of bugs and dirt. We can make a water filter to remove some dirt. Just put a paper towel in a funnel. If you don't have a funnel, use a sieve.

1. Mix some soil and water in a pitcher.

2. Put a piece of paper towel in a funnel or sieve.

3. Hold the funnel over another pitcher. Slowly pour the dirty water into it.

Let's Take a Closer Look!

The paper towel acts as a filter. It lets water through, but stops most of the soil and dirt. Our drinking water is filtered through gravel and sand at water treatment plants to get rid of dirt. Chemicals are also added to the filtered water to kill any harmful germs that might make us sick.

Try This!

Water is precious. Don't waste it! Remember to turn off the faucet when you are brushing your teeth!

Quick Warning!

Don't drink your filtered water. You can use it to water the garden or houseplants.

n many places, people can't just turn on the faucet to get water.

They have to walk miles to fetch clean water.

So Sticky!

Every liquid in the kitchen has its own different stickiness. If you try stirring a jar of water, you'll find that it is easier than stirring a jar of molasses. We can do a stickiness test on some liquids to see which is the stickiest one of all! You'll need some water, molasses, vegetable oil, and dishwashing soap.

1. Find four identical plastic cups. Pour a different liquid into each one. Fill them all to the same level.

2. Ask a friend to help. You will each need two marbles.

3. Drop a marble into each cup at the same time and from the same height.

4. Watch how long each one takes to reach the bottom of the cup.

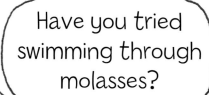
Have you tried swimming through molasses?

Let's Take a Closer Look!

The stickiness of a liquid, or how runny it is, is called **viscosity**. Thick, gooey liquids have high viscosity. It is hard to make things such as marbles or spoons move through them. Thin, runny liquids, such as water, have low viscosity. A marble moves quickly through them.

Did You Know?

Companies that make sauces like ketchup have to make sure that the viscosity is just right. Otherwise, the sauce will either stick in the bottle or come out too quickly!

Quick Quiz!

Do you think that milk has lower or higher viscosity than molasses?

Ketchup Coins

Make any pennies you have lying around look shiny and new with this experiment. Ketchup in a squeezable bottle is ideal. If yours isn't in a squeezable bottle, you can just put some ketchup in a small bowl and use a spoon instead.

1. Put some dirty pennies on a plate.

2. Squeeze or spoon a small amount of ketchup on each one.

3. Let the coins sit for about an hour.

4. Rinse off the ketchup.

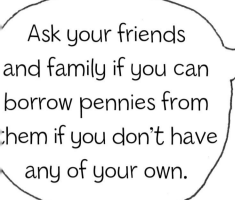

Ask your friends and family if you can borrow pennies from them if you don't have any of your own.

Try This!

Take one very dirty penny. Use a toothpick to put tiny blobs of ketchup on the coin to make eyes and a mouth. Let it sit and then rinse it off for a smiley coin!

Let's Take a Closer Look!

Copper coins get dirty and dull-looking. The ketchup has vinegar in it. Vinegar is something called an **acid**. It reacts with the dirty coating on the coin, leaving it nice and shiny.

Quick Fact

Lemons taste sour because they have acid in them.

Moldy Matters

You'll need two slices of bread and two chunks of cheese for this experiment. You won't be making sandwiches with it, though. We're going to find out why some food needs to be kept cold.

1. Seal each slice of bread and each chunk of cheese in a separate plastic bag.

2. Put a bag of bread and a bag of cheese in the fridge. Put the other bags on the windowsill.

3. Check them each day. Draw or write down what the bread and cheese look like each time.

Did You Know?

Food stored in a freezer can keep for several months. Put a piece of cheese and a piece of bread in the freezer. You will be able to eat a cheese sandwich when you are hungry in a few months!

I can't have a snack if it's kept in the fridge!

Quick Quiz!

o you think that the bread and eese will go moldy re or less quickly n hot weather ?

Let's Take a Closer Look!

The bread and cheese on the windowsill start growing blue-green mold after a few days. Mold grows on things that are no longer fresh. Food does not go bad as quickly in very cold places, like the fridge. Mold does not like the cold.

Melting Moments

When we are cooking, or heating, chopping, mixing, and stirring, we are really doing experiments. Get a grown-up to help you with this cooking experiment. Ask the grown-up which bowl to use for step 1, too.

1. Break up some chocolate and put it in a bowl over a pan of gently simmering water.

2. Stir it well as it becomes all runny and hot.

3. Spoon the melted chocolate over some cupcakes or cookies.

Try This!

Try to think of how other foods change when you heat them or they get warm. You could write down the changes or draw them.

Let's Take a Closer Look!

The chocolate chunks start out solid. As you heat them up, they melt, or become a liquid. When you spoon this liquid over the cookies or cupcakes, it cools down and becomes solid again.

Quick Warning!

Ask a grown-up to help you whenever you use the stove.

Always use pot holders to hold hot things like the bowl of chocolate.

Quick Quiz!

What happens to solid ice when it heats up?

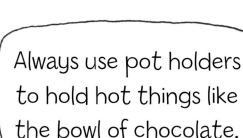

READ MORE

Brown, Cynthia Light. *Amazing Kitchen Chemistry Projects You Can Build Yourself.* White River Junction, Vermont: Nomad Press, 2008.

DK Publishing. *I'm a Scientist: Kitchen.* New York: DK Publishing, 2010.

GLOSSARY

acid (A-sud) Something that breaks down matter faster than water does.

carbon dioxide (KAR-bin dy-OK-syd) A colorless gas that people breathe out.

chemical reaction (KEH-mih-kul ree-AK-shun) What happens when matter is mixed together to cause changes.

gas (GAS) Matter that has no set shape or size.

liquid (LIH-kwed) Matter that flows.

solid (SOH-led) Matter that has a set shape and size.

viscosity (vis-KO-suh-tee) The thickness of a liquid.

Quiz Answers

Page 7 – Carbon dioxide

Page 11 – Oxygen

Page 17 – Lower

Page 21 – If it isn't in the fridge, food will go bad more quickly.

Page 23 – It melts and becomes liquid water.

INDEX

WEB SITES

For Web resources related to the subject of this book, go to: www.windmillbooks.com/weblinks and select this book's title.